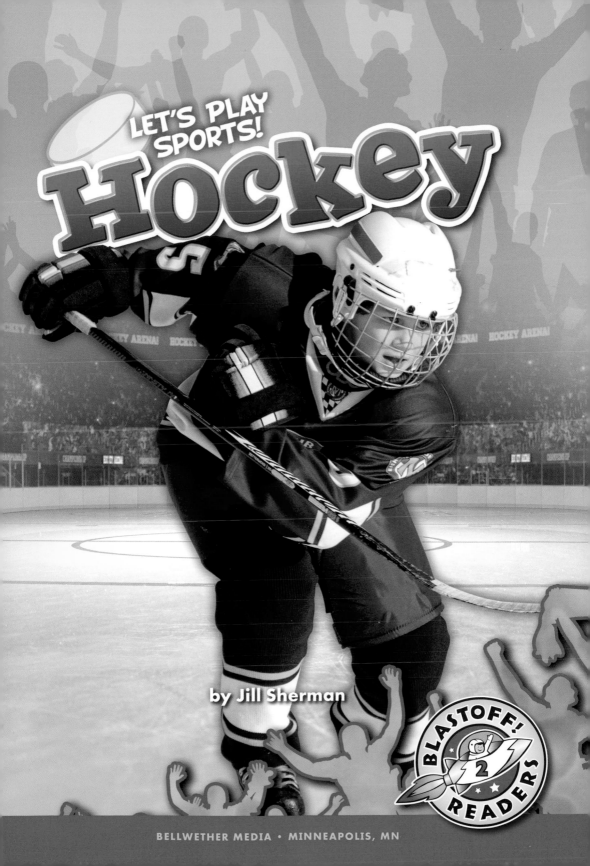

LET'S PLAY SPORTS!

# Hockey

by Jill Sherman

BLASTOFF! READERS
2

BELLWETHER MEDIA • MINNEAPOLIS, MN

Note to Librarians, Teachers, and Parents:

**Blastoff! Readers** are carefully developed by literacy experts and combine standards-based content with developmentally appropriate text.

**Level 1** provides the most support through repetition of high-frequency words, light text, predictable sentence patterns, and strong visual support.

**Level 2** offers early readers a bit more challenge through varied simple sentences, increased text load, and less repetition of high-frequency words.

**Level 3** advances early-fluent readers toward fluency through increased text and concept load, less reliance on visuals, longer sentences, and more literary language.

**Level 4** builds reading stamina by providing more text per page, increased use of punctuation, greater variation in sentence patterns, and increasingly challenging vocabulary.

**Level 5** encourages children to move from "learning to read" to "reading to learn" by providing even more text, varied writing styles, and less familiar topics.

Whichever book is right for your reader, Blastoff! Readers are the perfect books to build confidence and encourage a love of reading that will last a lifetime!

This edition first published in 2020 by Bellwether Media, Inc.

No part of this publication may be reproduced in whole or in part without written permission of the publisher. For information regarding permission, write to Bellwether Media, Inc., Attention: Permissions Department, 6012 Blue Circle Drive, Minnetonka, MN 55343.

Library of Congress Cataloging-in-Publication Data

Names: Sherman, Jill, author.
Title: Hockey / by Jill Sherman.
Description: Minneapolis, MN : Bellwether Media, Inc., 2020. | Series: Blastoff! Readers : Let's Play Sports! | Audience: Ages: 5-8. | Audience: Grades: K to grade 3. | Includes bibliographical references and index.
Identifiers: LCCN 2018058738 (print) | LCCN 2019004506 (ebook) | ISBN 9781618915429 (ebook) | ISBN 9781644870013 (hardcover : alk. paper)
Subjects: LCSH: Hockey–Juvenile literature.
Classification: LCC GV847.25 (ebook) | LCC GV847.25 .S456 2020 (print) | DDC 796.962–dc23
LC record available at https://lccn.loc.gov/2018058738

Editor: Rebecca Sabelko      Designer: Andrea Schneider

Printed in the United States of America, North Mankato, MN.

# Table of Contents

What Is Hockey?      4

What Are the Rules      8
for Hockey?

Hockey Gear      18

Glossary      22

To Learn More      23

Index      24

# What Is Hockey?

Hockey is a team sport played on an **ice rink**.

It is most popular in countries with long winters.

ice rink

Two teams of six players use hockey sticks to fight for the **puck**.

puck

## CHAMPION SPOTLIGHT
## WAYNE GRETZKY

- center forward
- National Hockey League (NHL)
- Accomplishments:
  - Won 4 Stanley Cup Finals
  - Scored NHL record 894 career goals
  - NHL MVP 9 times

Each team tries to score the most **goals**!

# What Are the Rules for Hockey?

A hockey game has 20-minute **periods**.

It begins when two players **face-off**. They try to take control of the puck.

face-off

offensive player

**Forwards** are **offensive** players. They use **slap shots** to score goals!

The center forward covers the middle of the ice. The wing forwards play near the **boards**.

boards

**Defenders** try to keep the puck away from their goal. They force the puck to the boards.

**Goalies** stay near the net. They block shots using all parts of their bodies.

goalie

defender

Defenders often slap
the puck across the ice rink.
This is called icing.

Icing stops the play.
Then two players face-off
to begin play again.

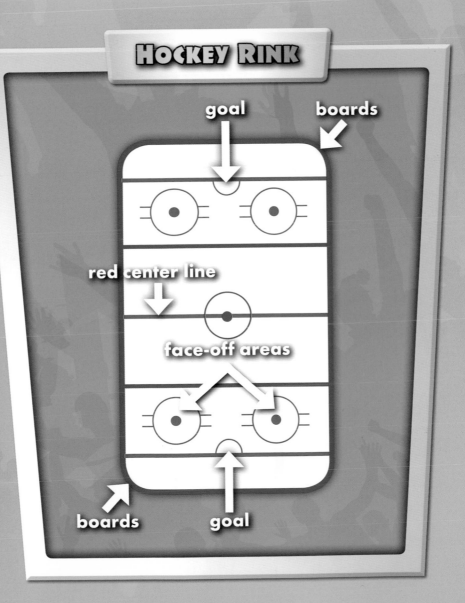

**HOCKEY RINK**

goal

boards

red center line

face-off areas

boards          goal

Sometimes players
break rules. They kick
the puck or trip someone.

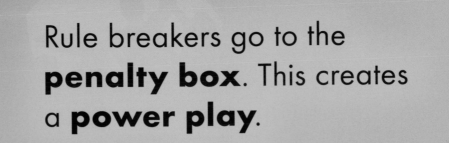

Rule breakers go to the
**penalty box**. This creates
a **power play**.

# Hockey Gear

Every hockey player needs skates.
Sharp blades let players move
and turn on the ice.

Players use a stick
to handle the puck.

**HOCKEY GEAR**

skates

stick

helmet

gloves

Each player also wears a helmet and pads.

Hockey is an action-packed sport. Keep an eye on the puck until the final horn!

# Glossary

**boards**—the walls around the ice rink

**defenders**—players who try to keep the other team from scoring

**face-off**—a way to begin play in which the puck is dropped between two players

**forwards**—players who play in attacking positions and try to score goals; forwards include the wings and the center positions.

**goalies**—players who guard the goal to keep other teams from scoring

**goals**—points scored when a puck goes into the hockey net

**ice rink**—a sheet of ice with a wall built around it; hockey is played on an ice rink.

**offensive**—related to the players whose aim is to score goals

**penalty box**—the area beside the ice rink where a player who has broken a rule sits for a certain amount of time

**periods**—the parts of a hockey game; a hockey game has three periods.

**power play**—when one team has more players on the ice

**puck**—a rubber disk used to play hockey

**slap shots**—powerful shots used to score goals

# To Learn More

Bechtel, Mark, and Beth Bugler. *My First Book of Hockey*. New York, N.Y.: Liberty Street, 2016.

Nagelhout, Ryan. *I Love Hockey*. New York, N.Y.: Gareth Stevens Publishing, 2015.

Schuh, Mari. *Hockey*. Mankato, Minn.: Amicus INK, 2018.

## ON THE WEB

# FACTSURFER

Factsurfer.com gives you a safe, fun way to find more information.

1. Go to www.factsurfer.com.

2. Enter "hockey" into the search box and click 🔍.

3. Select your book cover to see a list of related web sites.

# Index

boards, 11, 12
defenders, 12, 13, 14
face-off, 8, 9, 15
forwards, 10, 11
game, 8
gear, 19
goalies, 12
goals, 7, 10, 12
Gretzky, Wayne, 7
helmet, 20
ice rink, 4, 11, 14, 15, 18
icing, 14, 15
net, 12
offensive, 10
pads, 20

penalty box, 17
periods, 8
players, 6, 8, 10, 15, 16, 18, 19, 20
power play, 17
puck, 6, 8, 12, 14, 16, 19, 20
rules, 16, 17
score, 7, 10
shots, 10, 12
skates, 18
sticks, 6, 19
team, 4, 6, 7
winters, 4